Control of Hazardous Energy
Lockout/Tagout

U.S. Department of Labor
Elaine L. Chao, Secretary

Occupational Safety and Health Administration
John L. Henshaw, Assistant Secretary

OSHA 3120
2002 (Revised)

I0473156

Contents

How should I use this booklet?

This booklet presents OSHA's general requirements for controlling hazardous energy during service or maintenance of machines or equipment. It is not intended to replace or to supplement OSHA standards regarding the control of hazardous energy. After reading this booklet, employers and other interested parties are urged to review the OSHA standards on the control of hazardous energy to gain a complete understanding of the requirements regarding the control of hazardous energy. These standards, as well as other relevant resources, are identified throughout this publication.

What is "lockout/tagout"?

"Lockout/tagout" refers to specific practices and procedures to safeguard employees from the unexpected energization or startup of machinery and equipment, or the release of hazardous energy during service or maintenance activities.[1] This requires, in part, that a designated individual turns off and disconnects the machinery or equipment from its energy source(s) before performing service or maintenance and that the authorized employee(s) either lock or tag the energy-isolating device(s) to prevent the release of hazardous energy and take steps to verify that the energy has been isolated effectively. If the potential exists for the release of hazardous stored energy or for the reaccumulation of stored energy to a hazardous level, the employer must ensure that the employee(s) take steps to prevent injury that may result from the release of the stored energy.

Lockout devices hold energy-isolation devices in a safe or "off" position. They provide protection by preventing machines or equipment from becoming energized because they are

[1] The standard refers to servicing and maintaining "machines or equipment." Although the terms "machine" and "equipment" have distinct meanings, this booklet uses the term "machines" to refer both to machines and equipment. This is done for purposes of brevity only, and readers should not infer that it is intended to limit the scope of the standard. The term "equipment" is broad in scope and encompasses all types of equipment, including process equipment such as piping systems.

positive restraints that no one can remove without a key or other unlocking mechanism, or through extraordinary means, such as bolt cutters. Tagout devices, by contrast, are prominent warning devices that an authorized employee fastens to energy-isolating devices to warn employees not to reenergize the machine while he or she services or maintains it. Tagout devices are easier to remove and, by themselves, provide employees with less protection than do lockout devices.

Why do I need to be concerned about lockout/tagout?

Employees can be seriously or fatally injured if machinery they service or maintain unexpectedly energizes, starts up, or releases stored energy. OSHA's standard on the Control of Hazardous Energy (Lockout/Tagout), found in *Title 29 of the Code of Federal Regulations* (*CFR*) Part 1910.147, spells out the steps employers must take to prevent accidents associated with hazardous energy. The standard addresses practices and procedures necessary to disable machinery and prevent the release of potentially hazardous energy while maintenance or servicing activities are performed.

Two other OSHA standards also contain energy control provisions: *29 CFR* 1910.269 and 1910.333. In addition, some standards relating to specific types of machinery contain deenergization requirements—such as *29 CFR* 1910.179(l)(2)(i)(c) (requiring the switches to be "open and locked in the open position" before performing preventive maintenance on overhead and gantry cranes).[2] The provisions of Part 1910.147 apply in conjunction with these machine-specific standards to assure that employees will be adequately protected against hazardous energy.

---

[2] The standard provides a limited exception to the requirement that energy control procedures be documented. If an employer can demonstrate the existence of EACH of the eight elements listed in 1910.147(c)(4)(i), the employer is not required to document the energy control procedure. However, the exception terminates if circumstances change and ANY of the elements no longer exist.

How do I know if the OSHA standard applies to me?

If your employees service or maintain machines where the unexpected startup, energization, or the release of stored energy could cause injury, the standard likely applies to you. The standard applies to all sources of energy, including, but not limited to: mechanical, electrical, hydraulic, pneumatic, chemical, and thermal energy.

The standard does not cover electrical hazards from work on, near, or with conductors or equipment in electric utilization (premise wiring) installations, which are outlined by Subpart S of *29 CFR* Part 1910. You can find the specific lockout and tagout provisions for electrical shock and burn hazards in *29 CFR* Part 1910.333. Controlling hazardous energy in installations for the exclusive purpose of power generation, transmission, and distribution, including related equipment for communication or metering, is covered by *29 CFR* 1910.269.

The standard also does not cover the agriculture, construction, and maritime industries or oil and gas well drilling and servicing. Other standards concerning the control of hazardous energy, however, apply in many of these industries/situations.

When does the standard not apply to service and maintenance activities performed in industries covered by Part 1910?

The standard does not apply to general industry service and maintenance activities in the following situations, when:

- Exposure to hazardous energy is controlled completely by unplugging the equipment from an electric outlet and where the employee doing the service or maintenance has exclusive control of the plug. This applies only if electricity is the only form of hazardous energy to which employees may be exposed. This exception encompasses many portable hand tools and some cord and plug connected machinery and equipment.

- An employee performs hot-tap operations on pressurized pipelines that distribute gas, steam, water, or petroleum products, for which the employer shows the following:
  - Continuity of service is essential;
  - Shutdown of the system is impractical; and
  - The employee follows documented procedures and uses special equipment that provides proven, effective employee protection.

- The employee is performing minor tool changes or other minor servicing activities that are routine, repetitive, and integral to production, and that occur during normal production operations. In these cases, employees must have effective, alternative protection.

How does the standard apply to general industry service and maintenance operations?

The standard applies to the control of hazardous energy when employees are involved in service or maintenance activities such as constructing, installing, setting up, adjusting, inspecting, modifying, and maintaining or servicing machines or equipment. These activities include lubricating, cleaning or unjamming machines, and making adjustments or tool changes, where the employees may be exposed to hazardous energy.

If a service or maintenance activity is part of the normal production operation, the employee performing the servicing may be subjected to hazards not normally associated with the production operation itself. Although machine guarding provisions in Subpart O of *29 CFR* 1910 cover most normal production operations, workers doing service or maintenance activities during normal production operations must follow lockout/tagout procedures if they:

- Remove or bypass machine guards or other safety devices,

- Place any part of their bodies in or near a machine's point of operation, or

- Place any part of their bodies in a danger zone associated with machine operations.

Work involving minor tool changes and adjustments or other minor servicing activities that are routine, repetitive, and integral to the use of the production equipment and that occur during normal production operations are not covered by the lockout/tagout standard. This exception is limited, however, and applies only when economic considerations prevent the use of prescribed energy-isolation measures and when the employer provides and requires alternative measures to ensure effective, alternative protection.

Whenever the standard is applicable, the machinery must be shut off and isolated from its energy sources, and lockout or tagout devices must be applied to the energy-isolation devices. In addition, the authorized employee(s) must take steps to verify that he or she has effectively isolated the energy. When there is stored or residual energy, the authorized employee(s) must take steps to render that energy safe. If the possibility exists for reaccumulation of stored energy to hazardous levels, the employer must ensure that the worker(s) perform verification steps regularly to detect such reaccumulation before it has the potential to cause injury.

What are OSHA's requirements?

OSHA's standard establishes minimum performance requirements for controlling hazardous energy. The standard specifies that employers must establish an energy-control program to ensure that employees isolate machines from their energy sources and render them inoperative before any employee services or maintains them.

As part of an energy-control program, employers must:

*   Establish energy-control procedures for removing the energy supply from machines and for putting appropriate lockout or tagout devices on the energy-isolating devices to prevent unexpected reenergization. When appropriate, the procedure also must address stored or potentially reaccumulated energy;

*   Train employees on the energy-control program, including the safe application, use, and removal of energy controls; and

*   Inspect these procedures periodically (at least annually) to ensure that they are being followed and that they remain effective in preventing employee exposure to hazardous energy.

If employers use tagout devices on machinery that can be locked out, they must adopt additional measures to provide the same level of employee protection that lockout devices would provide. Within the broad boundaries of the standard, employers have the flexibility to develop programs and procedures that meet the needs of their individual workplaces and the particular types of machines being maintained or serviced.

What must an energy-control procedure include?

Employers must develop, document, and use procedures to control potentially hazardous energy.[3] The procedures explain what employees must know and do to control hazardous energy effectively when they service or maintain machinery. If this information is the same for the various machines used at a workplace, then a single energy-control procedure may suffice. For example, similar machines (those using the same type and magnitude of energy) that have the same or similar types of control measures can be covered by a single procedure. Employers must develop separate energy-control procedures if their workplaces have more variable conditions such as multiple energy sources, different power connections, or different control sequences that workers must follow to shut down various pieces of machinery.

The energy-control procedures must outline the scope, purpose, authorization, rules, and techniques that employees will use to control hazardous energy sources, as well as the means that will be used to enforce compliance. These procedures must provide employees at least the following information:

- A statement on how to use the procedures;

- Specific procedural steps to shut down, isolate, block, and secure machines;

- Specific steps designating the safe placement, removal, and transfer of lockout/tagout devices and identifying who has responsibility for the lockout/tagout devices; and

- Specific requirements for testing machines to determine and verify the effectiveness of lockout devices, tagout devices, and other energy-control measures.

---

[3] The standard provides a limited exception to the requirement that energy control procedures be documented. If an employer can demonstrate the existence of EACH of the eight elements listed in 1910.147(c)(4)(i), the employer is not required to document the energy control procedure. However, the exception terminates if circumstances change and ANY of the elements no longer exist.

In Appendix A to 1910.147, OSHA provides a *Typical Minimal Lockout Procedure* for employers to consult when preparing their own specific energy-control procedures. The outline is a nonmandatory guideline to help employers and employees comply with the standard. Nothing in the appendix adds to or detracts from any of the requirements in the standard.

What must workers do before they begin service or maintenance activities?

Before beginning service or maintenance, the following steps must be accomplished in sequence and according to the specific provisions of the employer's energy-control procedure:

(1) Prepare for shutdown;

(2) Shut down the machine;

(3) Disconnect or isolate the machine from the energy source(s);

(4) Apply the lockout or tagout device(s) to the energy-isolating device(s);

(5) Release, restrain, or otherwise render safe all potential hazardous stored or residual energy. If a possibility exists for reaccumulation of hazardous energy, regularly verify during the service and maintenance that such energy has not reaccumulated to hazardous levels; and

(6) Verify the isolation and deenergization of the machine.

What must workers do before they remove their lockout or tagout device and reenergize the machine?

Employees who work on deenergized machinery may be seriously injured or killed if someone removes lockout/tagout devices and reenergizes machinery without their knowledge. Thus, it is extremely important that all employees respect lockout and tagout devices and that only the person(s) who applied these devices remove them.

Before removing lockout or tagout devices, the employees must take the following steps in accordance with the specific provisions of the employer's energy-control procedure:

- Inspect machines or their components to assure that they are operationally intact and that nonessential items are removed from the area; and

- Check to assure that everyone is positioned safely and away from machines.

After removing the lockout or tagout devices but before reenergizing the machine, the employer must assure that all employees who operate or work with the machine, as well as those in the area where service or maintenance is performed, know that the devices have been removed and that the machine is capable of being reenergized. (See Sections 6(e) and (f) of *29 CFR* Part 1910.147 for specific requirements.) In the rare situation in which the employee who placed the lockout/tagout device is unable to remove that device, another person may remove it under the direction of the employer, provided that the employer strictly adheres to the specific procedures outlined in the standard. (See *29 CFR* 1910.147(e)(3).)

When do I use lockout and how do I do it?

You must use a lockout program (or tagout program that provides a level of protection equal to that achieved through lockout) whenever your employees engage in service or maintenance operations on machines that are capable of being locked out and that expose them to hazardous energy from unexpected energization, startup, or release of stored energy.

The primary way to prevent the release of hazardous energy during service and maintenance activities is by using energy-isolating devices such as manually operated circuit breakers, disconnect switches, and line valves and safety blocks. Lockout requires use of a lock or other lockout device to hold the energy-isolating device in a safe position to prevent machinery from becoming reenergized. Lockout also requires employees to follow an established procedure to ensure that machinery will not be reenergized until the same employee who placed the lockout device on the energy-isolating device removes it.

How can I determine if the energy-isolating device can be locked out?

An energy-isolating device is considered "capable of being locked out" if it meets one of the following requirements:

- Is designed with a hasp or other part to which you can attach a lock such as a lockable electric disconnect switch;

- Has a locking mechanism built into it; or

- Can be locked without dismantling, rebuilding, or replacing the energy-isolating device or permanently altering its energy-control capability, such as a lockable valve cover or circuit breaker blockout.

What do I do if I cannot lock out the equipment?

Sometimes it is not possible to lock out the energy-isolating device associated with the machinery. In that case, you must securely fasten a tagout device as close as safely possible to the energy-isolating device in a position where it will be immediately obvious to anyone attempting to operate the device. You also must meet all of the tagout provisions of the standard. The tag alerts employees to the hazard of reenergization and states that employees may not operate the machinery to which it is attached until the tag is removed in accordance with an established procedure.

What other options do I have?

If it is possible to lock out an energy-isolating device, employers must use lockout devices unless they develop, document, and use a tagout procedure that provides employees with a level of protection equal to that provided by a lockout device. In a tagout program, an employer can attain an equal level of protection by complying with all tagout-related provisions of the standard and using at least one added safety measure that prevents unexpected reenergization. Such measures might include removing an isolating circuit element, blocking a controlling switch, opening an extra disconnecting device, or removing a valve handle to minimize the possibility that machines might inadvertently be reenergized while employees perform service and maintenance activities.

When can tagout devices be used instead of lockout devices?

When an energy-isolating device cannot be locked out, the employer must modify or replace the energy-isolating device to make it capable of being locked out or use a tagout system. Whenever employers significantly repair, renovate, or modify machinery or install new or replacement machinery, however, they must ensure that the energy-isolating devices for the machinery are capable of being locked out.

Tagout devices may be used on energy-isolating devices that are capable of being locked out if the employer develops and implements the tagout in a way that provides employees with a level of protection equal to that achieved through a lockout system.

When using a tagout system, the employer must comply with all tagout-related provisions of the standard and train employees in the limitations of tags, in addition to providing normal hazardous energy control training for all employees.

What are the limitations of tagout devices?

A tagout device is a prominent warning that clearly states that the machinery being controlled must not be operated until the tag is removed in accordance with an established procedure. Tags are essentially warning devices and do not provide the physical restraint of a lock. Tags may evoke a false sense of security. For these reasons, OSHA considers lockout devices to be more secure and more effective than tagout devices in protecting employees from hazardous energy.

What are the requirements for lockout/tagout devices?

Whether lockout or tagout devices are used, they must be the only devices the employer uses in conjunction with energy-isolating devices to control hazardous energy. The employer must provide these devices and they must be singularly identified and not used for other purposes. In addition, they must have the following characteristics:

- Durable enough to withstand workplace conditions. Tagout devices must not deteriorate or become illegible even when used with corrosive components such as acid or alkali chemicals or in wet environments.

- Standardized according to color, shape, or size. Tagout devices also must be standardized according to print and format. Tags must be legible and understandable by all employees. They must warn employees about the hazards if the machine is energized, and offer employees clear instruction such as: "Do Not Start," "Do Not Open," "Do Not Close," "Do Not Energize," or "Do Not Operate."

- Substantial enough to minimize the likelihood of premature or accidental removal. Employees should be able to remove locks only by using excessive force with special tools such as bolt cutters or other metal-cutting tools. Tag attachments must be non-reusable, self-locking, and non-releasable, with a minimum unlocking strength of 50 pounds. Tags must be attachable by hand, and the device for attaching the tag should be a one-piece nylon cable tie or its equivalent so it can withstand all environments and conditions.

- Labeled to identify the specific employees authorized to apply and remove them.

What do employees need to know about lockout/tagout programs?

Training must ensure that employees understand the purpose, function, and restrictions of the energy-control program. Employers must provide training specific to the needs of "authorized," "affected," and "other" employees.

"Authorized" employees are those responsible for implementing the energy-control procedures or performing the service or maintenance activities. They need the knowledge and skills necessary for the safe application, use, and removal of energy-isolating devices. They also need training in the following:

- Hazardous energy source recognition;

- The type and magnitude of the hazardous energy sources in the workplace; and

- Energy-control procedures, including the methods and means to isolate and control those energy sources.

"Affected" employees (usually machine operators or users) are employees who operate the relevant machinery or whose jobs require them to be in the area where service or maintenance is performed. These employees do not service or maintain machinery or perform lockout/tagout activities. Affected employees must receive training in the purpose and use of energy-control procedures. They also need to be able to do the following:

- Recognize when the energy-control procedure is being used,

- Understand the purpose of the procedure, and

- Understand the importance of not tampering with lockout or tagout devices and not starting or using equipment that has been locked or tagged out.

All other employees whose work operations are or may be in an area where energy-control procedures are used must receive instruction regarding the energy-control procedure and the prohibition against removing a lockout or tagout device and attempting to restart, reenergize, or operate the machinery.

In addition, if tagout devices are used, all employees must receive training regarding the limitations of tags. (See *29 CFR* 1910.147(c)(7)(ii).)

When is training necessary?

The employer must provide initial training before starting service and maintenance activities and must provide retraining as necessary. In addition, the employer must certify that the training has been given to all employees covered by the standard. The certification must contain each employee's name and dates of training.

Employers must provide retraining for all authorized and affected employees whenever there is a change in the following:

- Job assignments,

- Machinery or processes that present a new hazard, or

- Energy-control procedures.

Retraining also is necessary whenever a periodic inspection reveals, or an employer has reason to believe, that shortcomings exist in an employee's knowledge or use of the energy-control procedure.

Control of Hazardous Energy (Lockout/Tagout)

What if I need power to test or position machines, equipment, or components?

OSHA allows the temporary removal of lockout or tagout devices and the reenergization of the machine only in limited situations for particular tasks that require energization—for example, when power is needed to test or position machines, equipment, or components. However, this temporary exception applies only for the limited time required to perform the particular task requiring energization. Employers must provide effective protection from hazardous energy when employees perform these operations. The following steps must be performed in sequence before reenergization:

1. Clear tools and materials from machines.

2. Clear employees from the area around the machines.

3. Remove the lockout or tagout devices as specified in the standard.

4. Energize the machine and proceed with testing or positioning.

5. Deenergize all systems, isolate the machine from the energy source, and reapply energy-control measures if additional service or maintenance is required.

The employer must develop, document, and use energy-control procedures that establish a sequence of actions to follow whenever reenergization is required as a part of a service or maintenance activity, since employees may be exposed to significant risks during these transition periods.

What if I use outside contractors for service or maintenance procedures?

If an outside contractor services or maintains machinery, the onsite employer and the contractor must inform each other of their respective lockout or tagout procedures. The onsite employer also must ensure that employees understand and comply with all requirements of the contractor's energy-control program(s).

What if a group performs service or maintenance activities?

When a crew, department, or other group performs service or maintenance, they must use a procedure that provides all employees a level of protection equal to that provided by a personal lockout or tagout device. Each employee in the group must have control over the sources of hazardous energy while he or she is involved in service and maintenance activities covered by the standard. Personal control is achieved when each authorized employee affixes a personal lockout/tagout device to a group lockout mechanism instead of relying on a supervisor or other person to provide protection against hazardous energy. Detailed requirements of individual responsibilities are provided in *29 CFR* 1910.147(f)(3)(ii)(A) through (D). Appendix C of OSHA Directive STD 1-7.3, *29 CFR* 1910.147, the Control of Hazardous Energy (Lockout/Tagout)-Inspection Procedures and Interpretive Guidance, (September 11, 1990), provides additional guidance.

What if a shift changes during machine service or maintenance?

Employers must make sure that there is a continuity of lockout or tagout protection. This includes the orderly transfer of lockout or tagout device protection between outgoing and incoming shifts to control hazardous energy. When lockout or tagout devices remain on energy-isolation devices from a previous shift, the incoming shift members must verify for themselves that the machinery is effectively isolated and deenergized.

How often do I need to review my lockout/tagout procedures?

Employees are required to review their procedures at least once a year to ensure that they provide adequate worker protection. As part of the review, employers must correct any deviations and inadequacies identified in the energy-control procedure or its application.

What does a review entail?

The periodic inspection is intended to assure that employees are familiar with their responsibilities under the procedure and continue to implement energy-control procedures properly. The inspector, who must be an authorized person not involved in using the particular control procedure being inspected, must be able to determine the following:

- Employees are following steps in the energy-control procedure;
- Employees involved know their responsibilities under the procedure; and
- The procedure is adequate to provide the necessary protection, and what changes, if any, are needed.

For a lockout procedure, the periodic inspection must include a review of each authorized employee's responsibilities under the energy-control procedure being inspected. Where tagout is used, the inspector's review also extends to affected employees because of the increased importance of their role in avoiding accidental or inadvertent activation of the machinery. In addition, the employer must certify that the designated inspectors perform periodic inspections. The certification must specify the following:

- Machine or equipment on which the energy-control procedure was used,
- Date of the inspection,
- Names of employees included in the inspection, and
- Name of the person who performed the inspection.

What additional information does OSHA provide about lockout/tagout?

To gain a more comprehensive understanding of the requirements for controlling hazardous energy, employers and other interested persons should review the following:

- OSHA standards with provisions regarding the control of hazardous energy such as *29 CFR* 1910.147, The control of hazardous energy (lockout/tagout); *29 CFR* 1910.269, Electric power generation, transmission, and distribution; and *29 CFR* 1910.333, Selection and use of work practices. Employers in the maritime, agriculture, and construction industries are urged to review the provisions for the control of hazardous energy contained in *29 CFR* Parts 1915, 1917, 1918, 1925, and 1926.

- The regulatory preambles to *29 CFR* 1910.147 (*54 Federal Register* 36644 (September 1, 1989)) and 1910.269 (*59 Federal Register* 4320 (January 31, 1994)), which contain comments from interested parties and OSHA's explanation for the provisions of the standards.

- OSHA instructions concerning the control of hazardous energy—Directive CPL 2-1.18A, Enforcement of the Electrical Power Generation, Transmission, and Distribution Standard (October 20, 1997) and OSHA Directive STD 1-7.3, *29 CFR* 1910.147, the Control of Hazardous Energy (Lockout/Tagout)-Inspection Procedures and Interpretive Guidance, (September 11, 1990).

- OSHA letters of interpretation regarding the application of standards concerning the control of hazardous energy.

Most of these documents are available on the OSHA website at www.osha.gov.

Additionally, OSHA offers a variety of web-based tools to help educate employers and employees about the lockout/tagout standard and how to apply it in their workplace. These include the following:

- The Lockout/Tagout Interactive Training Program, which includes a tutorial, five abstracts with a detailed discussion of major lockout/tagout issues involved, and interactive case studies;

- The Lockout/Tagout Plus Expert Advisor, an interactive, expert, diagnostic software package to help users understand and apply OSHA standards that protect workers from the release of hazardous energy; and

- The Lockout/Tagout electronic Compliance Assistant Tool (eCAT), an illustrated tool to help businesses identify and correct workplace hazards.

These tools are available on the OSHA website at www.osha.gov. For the Lockout/Tagout Interactive Training Program, click on **Technical Links**. For the Expert Advisor and eCAT, click on **eTools**.

Affected employee. An employee whose job requires him/her to operate or use a machine or equipment on which servicing or maintenance is being performed under lockout or tagout, or whose job requires him/her to work in an area in which such servicing or maintenance is being performed.

Authorized employee. A person who locks out or tags out machines or equipment in order to perform servicing or maintenance on that machine or equipment. An affected employee becomes an authorized employee when that employee's duties include performing servicing or maintenance covered under the standard.

Capable of being locked out. An energy-isolating device is capable of being locked out if it has a hasp or other means of attachment to which, or through which, a lock can be affixed, or it has a locking mechanism built into it. Other energy-isolating devices are capable of being locked out, if lockout can be achieved, without the need to dismantle, rebuild, or replace the energy-isolating device or permanently alter its energy control capability.

Energized. Connected to an energy source or containing residual or stored energy.

Energy-isolating device. A mechanical device that physically prevents the transmission or release of energy, including but not limited to the following: a manually operated electrical circuit breaker; a disconnect switch; a manually operated switch by which the conductors of a circuit can be disconnected from all ungrounded supply conductors, and in addition, no pole can be operated independently; a line valve; a block; and any similar device used to block or isolate energy. Push buttons, selector switches and other control circuit-type devices are not energy-isolating devices.

Energy source. Any source of electrical, mechanical, hydraulic, pneumatic, chemical, thermal, or other energy.

Hot tap. A procedure used in the repair, maintenance, and services activities, which involve welding on a piece of equipment (pipelines, vessels, or tanks) under pressure, in order to install connections or appurtenances. It is commonly used to replace or add sections of pipeline without the interruption of service for air, gas, water, steam, and petrochemical distribution systems.

Lockout. The placement of a lockout device on an energy-isolating device, in accordance with an established procedure, ensuring that the energy-isolating device and the equipment being controlled cannot be operated until the lockout device is removed.

Lockout device. A device that uses a positive means such as a lock, either key or combination type, to hold an energy-isolating device in the safe position and prevent the energizing of a machine or equipment. Included are blank flanges and bolted slip blinds.

Normal production operations. The utilization of a machine or equipment to perform its intended production function.

Servicing and/or maintenance. Workplace activities such as constructing, installing, setting up, adjusting, inspecting, modifying, and maintaining and/or servicing machines or equipment. These activities include lubricating, cleaning or unjamming machines or equipment and making adjustments or tool changes where the employee may be exposed to the unexpected energization or startup of the equipment or release of hazardous energy.

Setting up. Any work performed to prepare a machine or equipment to perform its normal production operation.

Tagout. The placement of a tagout device on an energy-isolating device, in accordance with an established procedure, to indicate that the energy-isolating device and the equipment being controlled may not be operated until the tagout device is removed.

Tagout device. A prominent warning device, such as a tag and a means of attachment, which can be securely fastened to an energy-isolating device in accordance with an established procedure, to indicate that the energy-isolating device and the equipment being controlled may not be operated until the tagout device is removed.

How can OSHA help me?

OSHA can provide extensive help through a variety of programs, including assistance about safety and health programs, state plans, workplace consultations, voluntary protection programs, strategic partnerships, training and education, and more.

How does safety and health program management assistance help employers and employees?

Effective management of worker safety and health protection is a decisive factor in reducing the extent and severity of work-related injuries and illnesses and their related costs. In fact, an effective safety and health program forms the basis of good worker protection and can save time and money —about $4 for every dollar spent—and increase productivity.

To assist employers and employees in developing effective safety and health programs, OSHA published recommended *Safety and Health Program Management Guidelines (Federal Register* 54(18):3908-3916, January 26, 1989). These voluntary guidelines can be applied to all worksites covered by OSHA.

The guidelines identify four general elements that are critical to the development of a successful safety and health management program:

- Management leadership and employee involvement,
- Worksite analysis,
- Hazard prevention and control, and
- Safety and health training.

The guidelines recommend specific actions under each of these general elements to achieve an effective safety and health program. The *Federal Register* notice is available online at www.osha.gov.

What are state plans?

State plans are OSHA-approved job safety and health programs operated by individual states or territories instead of Federal OSHA. The *Occupational Safety and Health Act of 1970 (OSH Act)* encourages states to develop and operate their own job safety and health plans and permits state enforcement of OSHA standards if the state has an approved plan. Once OSHA approves a state plan, it funds 50 percent of the program's operating costs. State plans must provide standards and enforcement programs, as well as voluntary compliance activities that are at least as effective as those of Federal OSHA.

There are 26 state plans: 23 cover both private and public (state and local governments) employment, and 3 (Connecticut, New Jersey, and New York) cover only the public sector. For more information on state plans, see the listing at the end of this publication, or visit OSHA's website at www.osha.gov.

How can consultation assistance help employers?

In addition to helping employers identify and correct specific hazards, OSHA's consultation service provides free, onsite assistance in developing and implementing effective workplace safety and health management systems that emphasize the prevention of worker injuries and illnesses.

Comprehensive consultation assistance provided by OSHA includes a hazard survey of the worksite and an appraisal of all aspects of the employer's existing safety and health management system. In addition, the service offers assistance to employers in developing and implementing an effective safety and health management system. Employers also may receive training and education services, as well as limited assistance away from the worksite.

Who can get consultation assistance and what does it cost?

Consultation assistance is available to small employers with fewer than 250 employees at a fixed site and no more than 500 corporatewide who want help in establishing and maintaining a safe and healthful workplace.

Funded largely by OSHA, the service is provided at no cost to the employer. Primarily developed for smaller employers with more hazardous operations, the consultation service is delivered by state governments employing professional safety and health consultants. No penalties are proposed or citations issued for hazards identified by the consultant. The employer's only obligation is to correct all identified serious hazards within the agreed-upon correction time frame.

Can OSHA assure privacy to an employer who asks for consultation assistance?

OSHA provides consultation assistance to the employer with the assurance that his or her name and firm and any information about the workplace will not be routinely reported to OSHA enforcement staff.

Can an employer be cited for violations after receiving consultation assistance?

If an employer fails to eliminate or control a serious hazard within the agreed-upon timeframe, the Consultation Project Manager must refer the situation to the OSHA enforcement office for appropriate action. This is a rare occurrence, however, since employers request the service for the expressed purpose of identifying and fixing hazards in their workplaces.

What incentives does OSHA provide for seeking consultation assistance?

Under the consultation program, certain exemplary employers may request participation in OSHA's Safety and Health Achievement Recognition Program (SHARP). Eligibility for participation in SHARP includes, but is not limited to, receiving a full-service, comprehensive consultation visit, correcting all identified hazards, and developing an effective safety and health management system.

Employers accepted into SHARP may receive an exemption from programmed inspections (not complaint or accident investigation inspections) for a period of 1 year initially, or 2 years upon renewal.

For more information concerning consultation assistance, see the list of consultation offices beginning on page 34, contact your regional or area OSHA office, or visit OSHA's website at www.osha.gov.

What are the Voluntary Protection Programs?

Voluntary Protection Programs (VPPs) represent one part of OSHA's effort to extend worker protection beyond the minimum required by OSHA standards. VPP—along with onsite consultation services, full-service area offices, and OSHA's Strategic Partnership Program (OSPP)—represents a cooperative approach which, when coupled with an effective enforcement program, expands worker protection to help meet the goals of the *OSH Act*.

How does the VPP work?

There are three levels of VPPs: Star, Merit, and Demonstration. All are designed to do the following:

- Recognize employers who have successfully developed and implemented effective and comprehensive safety and health management systems;

- Encourage these employers to continuously improve their safety and health management systems;

- Motivate other employers to achieve excellent safety and health results in the same outstanding way; and

- Establish a relationship between employers, employees, and OSHA that is based on cooperation.

How does VPP help employers and employees?

VPP participation can mean the following:

- Reduced numbers of worker fatalities, injuries, and illnesses;

- Lost-workday case rates generally 50 percent below industry averages;

- Lower workers' compensation and other injury- and illness-related costs;

- Improved employee motivation to work safely, leading to a better quality of life at work;

- Positive community recognition and interaction;

- Further improvement and revitalization of already-good safety and health programs; and

- A positive relationship with OSHA.

How does OSHA monitor VPP sites?

OSHA reviews an employer's VPP application and conducts a VPP Onsite Evaluation to verify that the safety and health management systems described are operating effectively at the site. OSHA conducts onsite evaluations on a regular basis, annually for participants at the Demonstration level, every 18 months for Merit, and every 3 to 5 years for Star. Each February, all participants must send a copy of their most recent annual evaluation to their OSHA regional office. This evaluation must include the worksite's record of injuries and illnesses for the past year.

Can OSHA inspect an employer who is participating in the VPP?

Sites participating in VPP are not scheduled for regular, programmed inspections. OSHA handles any employee complaints, serious accidents, or significant chemical releases that may occur at VPP sites according to routine enforcement procedures.

Additional information on VPP is available from OSHA national, regional, and area offices, listed beginning on page 34. Also, see Outreach at OSHA's website at www.osha.gov.

How can a partnership with OSHA improve worker safety and health?

OSHA has learned firsthand that voluntary, cooperative partnerships with employers, employees, and unions can be a useful alternative to traditional enforcement and an effective way to reduce worker deaths, injuries, and illnesses. This is especially true when a partnership leads to the development and implementation of a comprehensive workplace safety and health management system.

What is OSHA's Strategic Partnership Program (OSPP)?

OSHA Strategic Partnerships are alliances among labor, management, and government to foster improvements in workplace safety and health. These partnerships are voluntary, cooperative relationships between OSHA, employers, employee representatives, and others such as trade unions, trade and professional associations, universities, and other government agencies. OSPPs are the newest member of OSHA's family of cooperative programs.

What do OSPPs do?

These partnerships encourage, assist, and recognize the efforts of the partners to eliminate serious workplace hazards and achieve a high level of worker safety and health. Whereas OSHA's Consultation Program and VPP entail one-on-one relationships between OSHA and individual worksites, most strategic partnerships seek to have a broader impact by building cooperative relationships with groups of employers and employees.

What are the different kinds of OSPPs?

There are two major types:

- Comprehensive, which focuses on establishing comprehensive safety and health management systems at partnering worksites; and

- Limited, which helps identify and eliminate hazards associated with worker deaths, injuries, and illnesses, or have goals other than establishing comprehensive worksite safety and health programs.

OSHA is interested in creating new OSPPs at the national, regional, and local levels. OSHA also has found limited partnerships to be valuable. Limited partnerships might address the elimination or control of a specific industry hazard.

What are the benefits of participation in the OSPP?

Like VPP, OSPP can mean the following:

- Fewer worker fatalities, injuries, and illnesses;

- Lower workers' compensation and other injury- and illness-related costs;

- Improved employee motivation to work safely, leading to a better quality of life at work and enhanced productivity;

- Positive community recognition and interaction;

- Development of or improvement in safety and health management systems; and

- Positive interaction with OSHA.

For more information about this program, contact your nearest OSHA office or go to the agency website at www.osha.gov.

Does OSHA have occupational safety and health training for employers and employees?

Yes. The OSHA Training Institute in Des Plaines, IL, provides basic and advanced training and education in safety and health for federal and state compliance officers, state consultants, other federal agency personnel, and private-sector employers, employees, and their representatives.

Institute courses cover diverse safety and health topics including electrical hazards, machine guarding, personal protective equipment, ventilation, and ergonomics. The facility includes classrooms, laboratories, a library, and an audiovisual unit. The laboratories contain various demonstrations and equipment, such as power presses, woodworking and welding shops, a complete industrial ventilation unit, and a sound demonstration laboratory. More than 57 courses dealing with subjects such as safety and health in the construction industry and methods of compliance with OSHA standards are available for personnel in the private sector.

In addition, OSHA's 73 area offices are full-service centers offering a variety of informational services such as personnel for speaking engagements, publications, audiovisual aids on workplace hazards, and technical advice.

Does OSHA give money to organizations for training and education?

OSHA awards grants through its Susan Harwood Training Grant Program to nonprofit organizations to provide safety and health training and education to employers and workers in the workplace. The grants focus on programs that will educate workers and employers in small business (fewer than 250 employees), train workers and employers about new OSHA standards, or a high-risk activities or hazards. Grants are awarded for 1 year and may be renewed for an additional 12 months depending on whether the grantee has performed satisfactorily.

OSHA expects each organization awarded a grant to develop a training and/or education program that addresses a safety and health topic named by OSHA, recruit workers and employers for the training, and conduct the training. Grantees are also expected to follow up with people who have been trained to find out what changes were made to reduce the hazards in their workplaces as a result of the training.

Each year OSHA has a national competition that is announced in the *Federal Register* and on the Internet at www.osha-slc.gov/Training/sharwood/sharwood html. If you do not have access to the Internet, you can contact the OSHA Office of Training and Education, 1555 Times Drive, Des Plaines, IL 60018, (847) 297–4810, for more information.

Does OSHA have other assistance materials available?

Yes. OSHA has a variety of materials and tools available on its website at www.osha.gov. These include eTools, Expert Advisors, Electronic Compliance Assistance Tools (eCATS), Technical Links, regulations, directives, publications, videos, and other information for employers and employees. OSHA's software programs and compliance assistance tools walk you through challenging safety and health issues and common problems to find the best solutions for your workplace. OSHA's comprehensive publications program includes more than 100 titles to help you understand OSHA requirements and programs.

OSHA's CD-ROM includes standards, interpretations, directives, and more and can be purchased on CD-ROM from the U.S. Government Printing Office. To order, write to the Superintendent of Documents, U.S. Government Printing Office, Washington, DC 20402, or phone (202) 512–1800. Specify *OSHA Regulations, Documents and Technical Information on CD-ROM (ORDT)*, GPO Order No. S/N 729-013-00000-5.

What do I do in case of an emergency or to file a complaint?

To report an emergency, file a complaint, or seek OSHA advice, assistance, or products, call (800) 321–OSHA or contact your nearest OSHA regional or area office listed at the end of this publication. The teletypewriter (TTY) number is (877) 889–5627.

You can also file a complaint online and obtain more information on OSHA federal and state programs by visiting OSHA's website at www.osha.gov.

For more information on grants, training, and education, write: OSHA Training Institute, Office of Training and Education, 1555 Times Drive, Des Plaines, IL 60018; call (847) 297-4810; or see **Outreach** on OSHA's website at www.osha.gov.

OSHA Regional Offices

Region I
(CT,* MA, ME, NH, RI, VT*)
JFK Federal Building
Room E-340
Boston, MA 02203
Telephone: (617) 565–9860

Region II
(NJ,* NY,* PR,* VI*)
201 Varick Street
Room 670
New York, NY 10014
Telephone: (212) 337–2378

Region III
(DC, DE, MD,* PA, VA,* WV)
The Curtis Center—Suite 740 West
170 S. Independence Mall West
Philadelphia, PA 19106-3309
Telephone: (215) 861–4900

Region IV
(AL, FL, GA, KY,* MS, NC,*
SC,* TN*)
Atlanta Federal Center
61 Forsyth Street, SW, Room 6T50
Atlanta, GA 30303
Telephone: (404) 562–2300

Region V
(IL, IN,* MI,* MN,* OH, WI)
230 South Dearborn Street
Room 3244
Chicago, IL 60604
Telephone: (312) 353–2220

Region VI
(AR, LA, MN,* OK, TX)
525 Griffin Street
Room 602
Dallas, TX 75202
Telephone: (214) 767–4731

Region VII
(IA,* KS, MO, NE)
City Center Square
1100 Main Street, Suite 800
Kansas City, MO 64105
Telephone: (816) 426–5861

Region VIII
(CO, MT, ND, SD, UT,* WY*)
1999 Broadway
Suite 1690
Denver, CO 80802-5716
Telephone: (303) 844–1600

Region IX
(American Samoa, AZ,* CA,*
Guam, HI,* NV,*
Commonwealth of the
Northern Mariana Islands)
71 Stevenson Street
4th Floor
San Francisco, CA 94105
Telephone: (415) 975–4310

Region X
(AK,* ID, OR,* WA*)
1111 Third Avenue
Suite 715
Seattle, WA 98101-3212
Telephone: (206) 553–5930

* These states and territories operate their own OSHA-approved job safety and health programs (Connecticut, New Jersey, and New York plans cover public employees only). States with approved programs must have a standard that is identical to, or at least as effective as, the federal standard.

OSHA Area Offices

Anchorage, AK
(907) 271–5152

Birmingham, AL
(205) 731–1534

Mobile, AL
(334) 441–6131

Little Rock, AR
(501) 324–6291 (5818)

Phoenix, AZ
(602) 640–2348

Sacramento, CA
(916) 566–7471

San Diego, CA
(619) 557–5909

Denver, CO
(303) 844–5285

Englewood, CO
(303) 843–4500

Bridgeport, CT
(203) 579–5581

Hartford, CT
(860) 240–3152

Wilmington, DE
(302) 573–6518

Fort Lauderdale, FL
(954) 424–0242

Jacksonville, FL
(904) 232–2895

Tampa, FL
(813) 626–1177

Savannah, GA
(912) 652–4393

Smyrna, GA
(770) 984–8700

Tucker, GA
(770) 493–6644/6742/8419

Des Moines, IA
(515) 284–4794

Boise, ID
(208) 321–2960

Calumet City, IL
(708) 891–3800

Des Plaines, IL
(847) 803–4800

Fairview Heights, IL
(618) 632–8612

North Aurora, IL
(630) 896–8700

Peoria, IL
(309) 671–7033

Indianapolis, IN
(317) 226–7290

Wichita, KS
(316) 269–6644

Frankfort, KY
(502) 227–7024

Baton Rouge, LA
(225) 389–0474 (0431)

Braintree, MA
(617) 565–6924

Methuen, MA
(617) 565–8110

Springfield, MA
(413) 785–0123

Linthicum, MD
(410) 865–2055/2056

Augusta, ME
(207) 622–8417

Bangor, ME
(207) 941–8177

Portland, ME
(207) 780–3178

Lansing, MI
(517) 327–0904

Minneapolis, MN
(612) 664–5460

Kansas City, MO
(816) 483–9531

St. Louis, MO
(314) 425–4289

Jackson, MS
(601) 965–4606

Billings, MT
(406) 247–7494

Raleigh, NC
(919) 856–4770

Bismark, ND
(701) 250–4521

Omaha, NE
(402) 221–3182

Concord, NH
(603) 225–1629

Avenel, NJ
(732) 750–3270

Hasbrouck Heights, NJ
(201) 288–1700

Marlton, NJ
(609) 757–5181

Parsippany, NJ
(973) 263–1003

Albuquerque, NM
(505) 248–5302

Carson City, NV
(775) 885–6963

Albany, NY
(518) 464–4338

Bayside, NY
(718) 279–9060

Bowmansville, NY
(716) 684–3891

New York, NY
(212) 466–2482

North Syracuse, NY
(315) 451–0808

Tarrytown, NY
(914) 524–7510

Westbury, NY
(516) 334–3344

Cincinnati, OH
(513) 841–4132

Cleveland, OH
(216) 522–3818

Columbus, OH
(614) 469–5582

Toledo, OH
(419) 259–7542

Oklahoma City, OK
(405) 231–5351 (5389)

Portland, OR
(503) 326–2251

Allentown, PA
(610) 776–0592

Erie, PA
(814) 833–5758

Harrisburg, PA
(717) 782–3902

Philadelphia, PA
(215) 597–4955

Pittsburgh, PA
(412) 395–4903

Wilkes–Barre, PA
(570) 826–6538

Guaynabo, PR
(787) 277–1560

Providence, RI
(401) 528–4669

Columbia, SC
(803) 765–5904

Nashville, TN
(615) 781–5423

Austin, TX
(512) 916–5783 (5788)

Corpus Christi, TX
(512) 888–3420

Dallas, TX
(214) 320–2400 (2558)

El Paso, TX
(915) 534–6251

Fort Worth, TX
(817) 428–2470 (485–7647)

Houston, TX
(281) 591–2438 (2787)

Houston, TX
(281) 286–0583/0584 (5922)

Lubbock, TX
(806) 472–7681 (7685)

Salt Lake City, UT
(801) 530–6901

Norfolk, VA
(757) 441–3820

Bellevue, WA
(206) 553–7520

Appleton, WI
(920) 734–4521

Eau Claire, WI
(715) 832–9019

Madison, WI
(608) 264–5388

Milwaukee, WI
(414) 297–3315

Charleston, WV
(304) 347–5937

Anchorage, AK
(907) 269–4957

Tuscaloosa, AL
(205) 348–3033

Little Rock, AR
(501) 682–4522

Phoenix, AZ
(602) 542–1695

Sacramento, CA
(916) 574–2555

Fort Collins, CO
(970) 491–6151

Wethersfield, CT
(860) 566–4550

Washington, DC
(202) 541–3727

Wilmington, DE
(302) 761–8219

Tampa, FL
(813) 974–9962

Atlanta, GA
(404) 894–2643

Tiyam, GU
9–1–(671) 475–1101

Honolulu, HI
(808) 586–9100

Des Moines, IA
(515) 281–7629

Boise, ID
(208) 426–3283

Chicago, IL
(312) 814–2337

Indianapolis, IN
(317) 232–2688

Topeka, KS
(785) 296–7476

Frankfort, KY
(502) 564–6895

Baton Rouge, LA
(225) 342–9601

West Newton, MA
(617) 727–3982

Laurel, MD
(410) 880–4970

Augusta, ME
(207) 624–6460

Lansing, MI
(517) 322–1809

Saint Paul, MN
(651) 297–2393

Jefferson City, MO
(573) 751–3403

Jackson, MS
(601) 987–3981

Helena, MT
(406) 444–6418

Raleigh, NC
(919) 807–2905

Bismarck, ND
(701) 328–5188

Lincoln, NE
(402) 471–4717

Concord, NH
(603) 271–2024

Trenton, NJ
(609) 292–3923

Santa Fe, NM
(505) 827–4230

Albany, NY
(518) 457–2238

Henderson, NV
(702) 486–9140

Columbus, OH
(614) 644–2631

Oklahoma City, OK
(405) 528–1500

Salem, OR
(503) 378–3272

Indiana, PA
(724) 357–2396

Hato Rey, PR
(787) 754–2171

Providence, RI
(401) 222–2438

Columbia, SC
(803) 734–9614

Brookings, SD
(605) 688–4101

Nashville, TN
(615) 741–7036

Austin, TX
(512) 804–4640

Salt Lake City, UT
(801) 530–6901

Richmond, VA
(804) 786–6359

Christiansted St. Croix, VI
(809) 772–1315

Montepilier, VT
(802) 828–2765

Olympia, WA
(360) 902–5638

Madison, WI
(608) 266–9383

Waukesha, WI
(262) 523–3044

Charleston, WV
(304) 558–7890

Cheyenne, WY
(307) 777–7786

Juneau, AK
(907) 465–2700

Phoenix, AZ
(602) 542–5795

San Francisco, CA
(415) 703–5050

Wethersfield, CT
(860) 263–6505

Honolulu, HI
(808) 586–8844

Des Moines, IA
(515) 281–3447

Indianapolis, ID
(317) 232–2378

Indianapolis, IN
(317) 232–3325

Frankfort, KY
(502) 564–3070

Baltimore, MD
(410) 767–2215

Lansing, MI
(517) 322–1814

St. Paul, MN
(651) 284–5010

Raleigh, NC
(919) 807–2900

Trenton, NJ
(609) 292–2975

Santa Fe, NM
(505) 827–2850

Carson City, NV
(775) 684–7260

Salem, OR
(503) 378–3272

Hato Rey, PR
(787) 754–2119

Columbia, SC
(803) 896–4300

Nashville, TN
(615) 741–2582

Salt Lake City, UT
(801) 530–6901

Richmond, VA
(804) 786–2377

Christiansted, St. Croix, VI
(340) 773–1990

Montpelier VT
(802) 828–2288

Olympia, WA
(360) 902–4200
(360) 902–5430

Cheyenne, WY
(307) 777–7786